PAPER BOXES

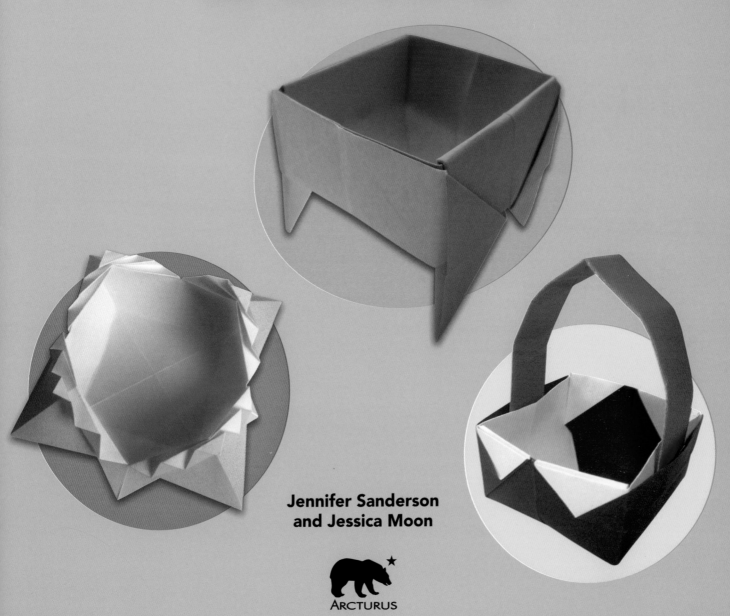

Jennifer Sanderson
and Jessica Moon

ARCTURUS

This edition first published in 2015 by Arcturus Publishing

Distributed by Black Rabbit Books
P.O. Box 3263
Mankato
Minnesota MN 56002

Models and photography: Jessica Moon
Text: Jennifer Sanderson
Editors: Becca Clunes and Joe Harris
Designer: Jessica Moon

Library of Congress Cataloging-in-Publication Data

Sanderson, Jennifer, author.
 Paper boxes / Jennifer Sanderson & Jessica Moon.
     pages cm. -- (Origami and papercraft)
 Audience: Grades 4 to 6.
 Includes bibliographical references and index.
 ISBN 978-1-78404-083-3
1. Origami--Juvenile literature. 2. Paper work--Juvenile literature. 3. Box making--Juvenile literature. I.
Moon, Jessica, designer. II. Title.
 TT872.5.S263 2015
 736.982--dc23

                                2013048126

Printed in China

SL004077US
Supplier 29, Date 0514, Print Run 3405

Contents

Introduction

Origami has been popular in Japan for hundreds of years and is now loved all around the world. You can make great models with just one sheet of paper and this book shows you how!

The paper used in origami is thin but strong, so that it can be folded many times. It is usually colored on one side. Alternatively, you can use ordinary scrap paper but make sure it's not too thick.

Origami models often share the same folds and basic designs, known as "bases". This introduction explains some of the folds and bases that you will need for the projects in this book. When making the models, follow the key below to find out what the lines and arrows mean. Always crease your paper well!

MOUNTAIN FOLD

To make a mountain fold, fold the paper so that the crease is pointing up toward you, like a mountain.

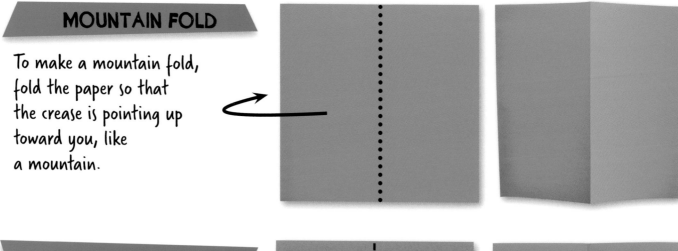

VALLEY FOLD

To make a valley fold, fold the paper the other way, so that the crease is pointing away from you, like a valley.

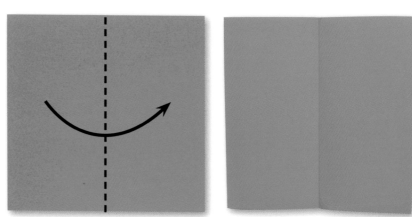

INSIDE REVERSE FOLD

An inside reverse fold is useful if you want to flatten the shape of part of your model.

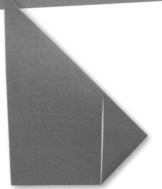

Open

1 Practice by first folding a piece of paper diagonally in half. Make a valley fold on one point and crease.

2 It's important to make sure that the paper is creased well. Run your finger over the crease two or three times.

3 Unfold and open up the corner slightly. Refold the crease nearest to you into a mountain fold.

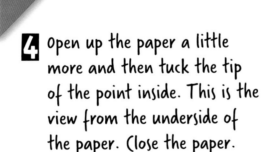

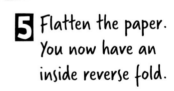

4 Open up the paper a little more and then tuck the tip of the point inside. This is the view from the underside of the paper. Close the paper.

5 Flatten the paper. You now have an inside reverse fold.

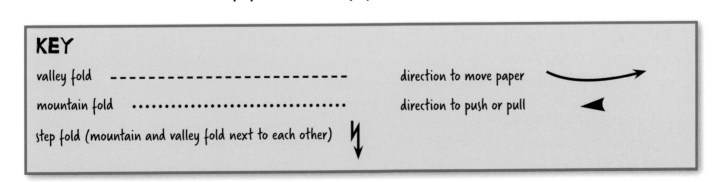

KEY

valley fold – – – – – – – – – – –	direction to move paper ⟶
mountain fold ··················	direction to push or pull ◄
step fold (mountain and valley fold next to each other) ↯	

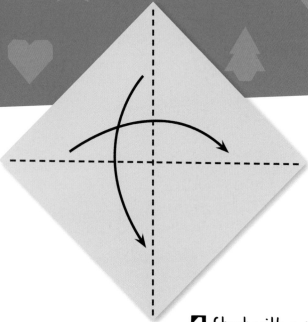

1 Start with a square of paper, with the point toward you. Make two diagonal valley folds.

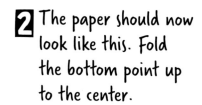

2 The paper should now look like this. Fold the bottom point up to the center.

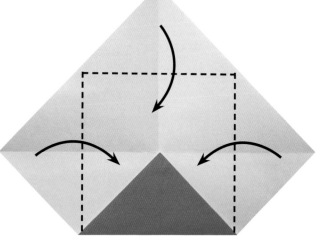

3 Repeat step 2 with the three remaining points.

4 You now have a blintz base.

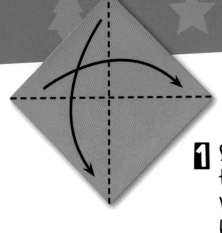

1 Start with the point turned toward you. Valley fold diagonally both ways.

2 The paper should look like this. Now turn it over.

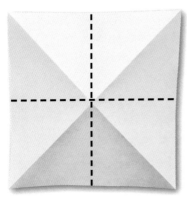

3 Valley fold along the horizontal and vertical lines.

4 The paper should now look like this. Turn it so that one of the points is facing you.

 Push

Push

5 Hold the paper by opposite diagonal corners. Push the two corners together so that the shape begins to collapse.

6 Flatten the top of the paper into a square shape. You now have a square base.

Pen Holder

Keep your pens neat and tidy in this handy origami pen holder. You'll never lose a pen again!

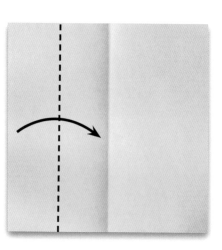

That's useful!

START WITH YOUR PAPER COLORED SIDE DOWN

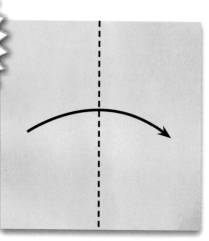

1 Valley fold the paper in half, crease well, then unfold.

2 Valley fold the left side into the center. Crease well and then unfold.

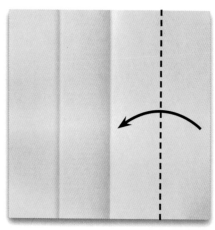

3 Do the same to the right side.

4 Valley fold the top corner into the center of the paper.

5 Valley fold the top corner of the far right panel.

6 Valley fold the right panel into the center of the paper.

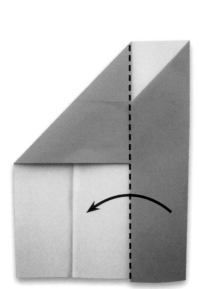

7 Valley fold the right panel again.

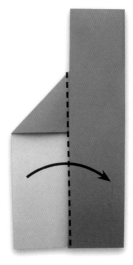

8 Valley fold the left panel over to the right.

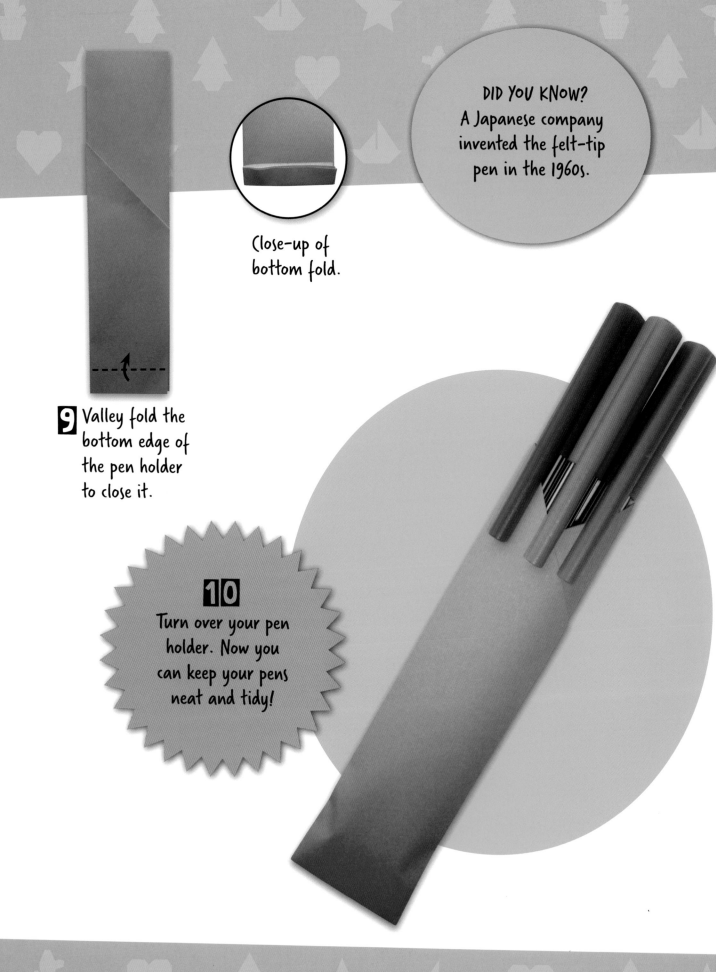

Close-up of
bottom fold.

DID YOU KNOW?
A Japanese company
invented the felt-tip
pen in the 1960s.

9 Valley fold the
bottom edge of
the pen holder
to close it.

10
Turn over your pen
holder. Now you
can keep your pens
neat and tidy!

Star Box

This pretty box draws attention to its contents. You could use it to store beads, paper clips, or buttons.

START WITH A SQUARE BASE

A fun gift!

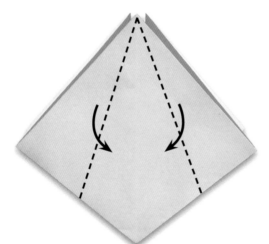

1 You will need to make your square base so that the color is on the inside. Turn it so that the open part is at the top. Valley fold the two top flaps to meet the center line.

2 Your model should now look like this. Turn it over and repeat step 1.

3 Valley fold each flap and crease it well.

4 Gently tease out the top right flap, as shown. Flatten the flap. Repeat on the left flap.

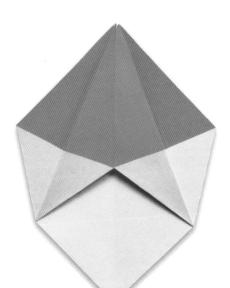

5 Your model should now look like this. Turn over the paper.

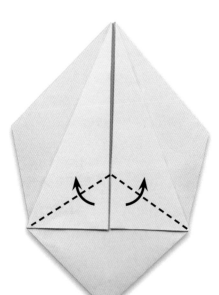

6 Valley fold the top flaps.

7 Your model should look like this. Repeat step 4.

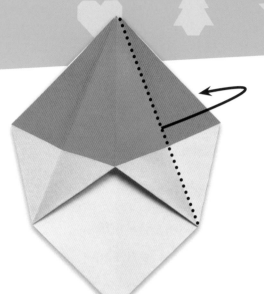

8 Take the top-right flap and mountain fold it behind itself.

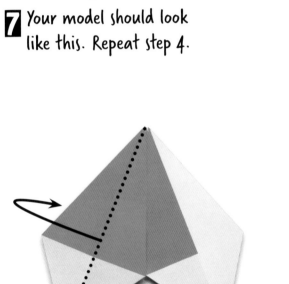

9 Do the same on the left side.

10 Your model now looks like this. Turn it over and repeat steps 8 and 9.

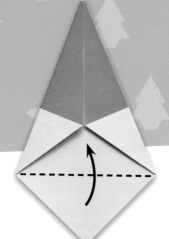

11 Valley fold the bottom, and crease well along the fold. Unfold.

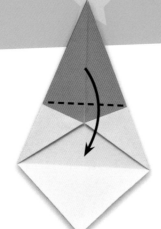

12 Valley fold down the top flap.

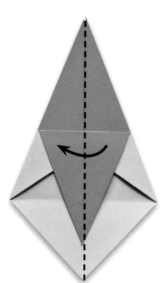

13 Valley fold the top right flap over to the left. Then, repeat step 12.

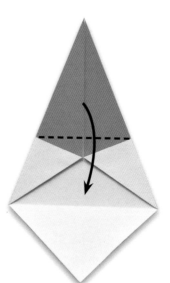

14 Turn over the paper and repeat steps 12 and 13.

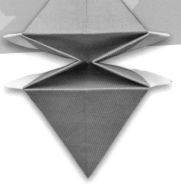

15 Your model should now look like this.

16 Turn the model so that it looks like this from above. Pull out the four pointed flaps.

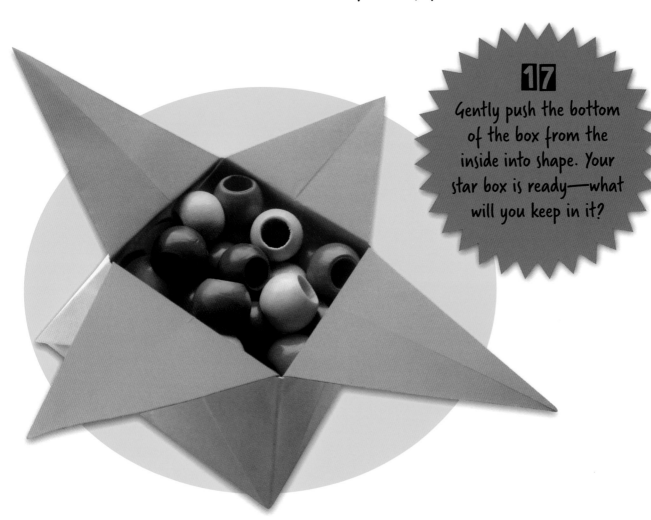

17 Gently push the bottom of the box from the inside into shape. Your star box is ready—what will you keep in it?

Card Holder

This easy-to-make box will keep all your cards neat and tidy. You can also use it to keep important pieces of paper safe.

Cool!

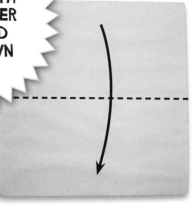

START WITH YOUR PAPER COLORED SIDE DOWN

1 Valley fold your paper in half, crease well, then unfold it.

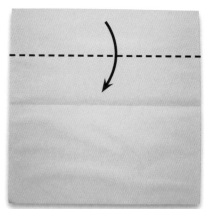

2 Valley fold the top side into the center. Crease the paper, then unfold it.

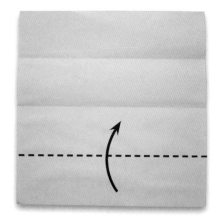

3 Valley fold the bottom side into the center. Crease and then unfold.

4 Valley fold the top left corner of the top panel.

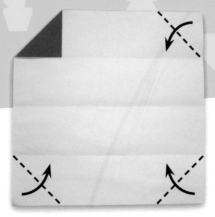

5 Do the same on the
three remaining corners.

6 Valley fold the top panel
into the center of the paper.

7 Valley fold the bottom panel
into the center of the paper.

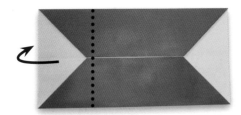

8 Mountain fold the left
side, just to the right
of the V-shape.

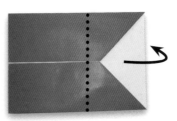

9 Mountain fold the right side, just
to the left of the V-shape but so
that it creates an overlap.

Tuck

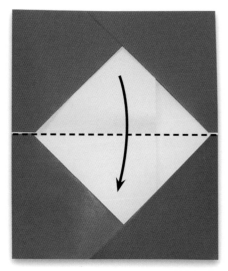

Close-up of overlap.

10 Turn over your model. Tuck the left side into the triangles on the right, so that they overlap.

11 Valley fold in half at the center.

12 Your card holder is now ready to use.

Pleated Box

You can use this striking box to store anything, from buttons and beads to candy.

START WITH A BLINTZ BASE

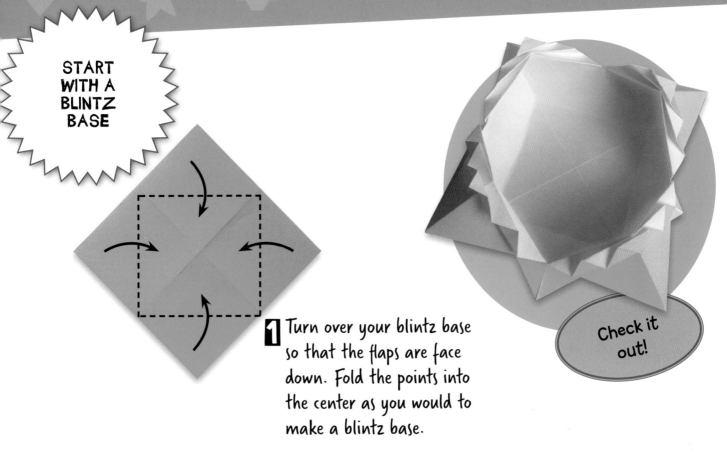

Check it out!

1 Turn over your blintz base so that the flaps are face down. Fold the points into the center as you would to make a blintz base.

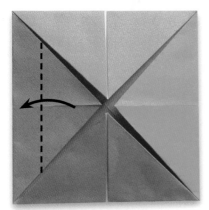

2 Valley fold the left flap to the left, so that it overlaps the left edge.

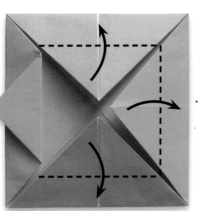

3 Do the same with the three remaining flaps then turn over the paper.

4 Valley fold the top left flap diagonally to the top left corner.

5 Valley fold the corner again into the center to make the first pleat.

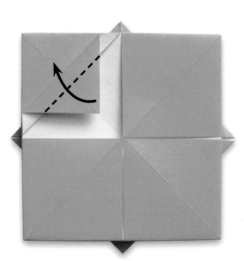

6 Repeat with a valley fold toward the outer corner.

7 Continue the pleat with a valley fold toward the center.

8 Continue the pleat with a valley fold toward the outer corner.

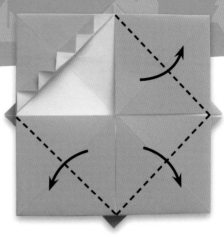

9 Repeat steps 5 to 8 on the three remaining corners.

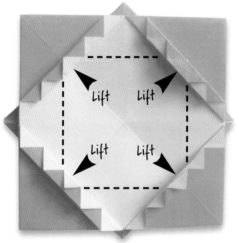

Lift Lift

Lift Lift

10 Insert your fingers into the corners to give your box shape. Fold along the lines to lift the sides and create a square base for your box.

11 Keep all your buttons safe in your pretty, pleated box.

Standing Container

This box can stand up on your desk, so it is great for storing stationery such as paper clips, marker pens, and erasers.

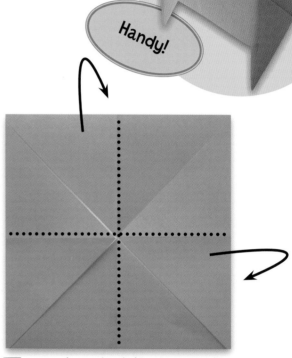

Handy!

START WITH A BLINTZ BASE

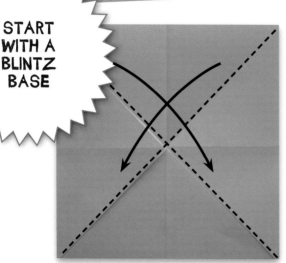

1 Put your blintz base flap-side up. Valley fold the diagonal folds again. Crease well.

2 Mountain fold the horizontal and vertical folds. Crease well.

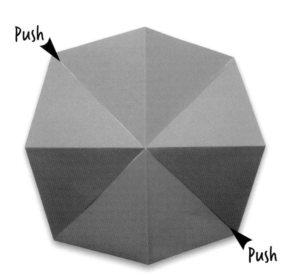

Push

Push

3 Collapse the paper into a square base, using page 7 as a guide.

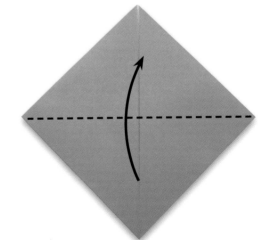

4 Place the paper so that the open side is at the bottom. Valley fold the bottom flap in half. Crease well and unfold.

Pull ◄ ► Pull

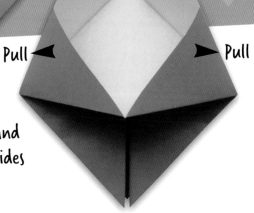

Pull ◄ ► Pull

5 Prise open the center and carefully fold up the sides to make an opening.

6 Continue to pull the model as shown.

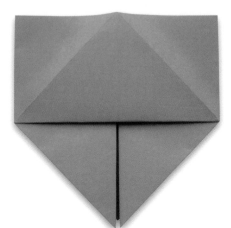

7 Your model should look like this. Turn over the paper and repeat steps 4, 5, and 6 on the other side.

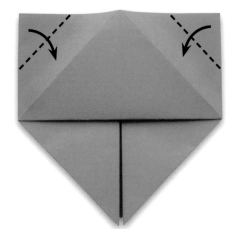

8 Valley fold the top corners, crease, and then unfold.

Open

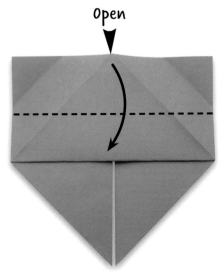

9 Gently prise open the top flap, valley fold horizontally, and flatten.

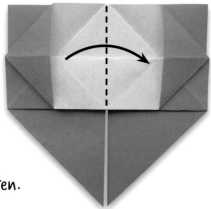

10 Valley fold the left flap over to the right hand side.

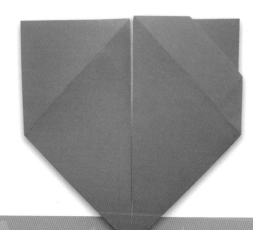

11 Your model should now look like this. Turn over the paper and repeat steps 8, 9, and 10 on the other side.

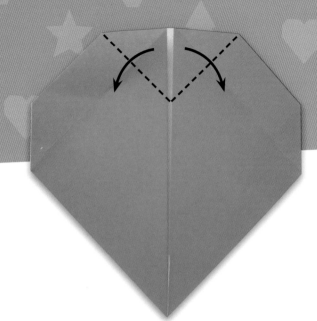

12 Diagonally valley fold the top center flaps.

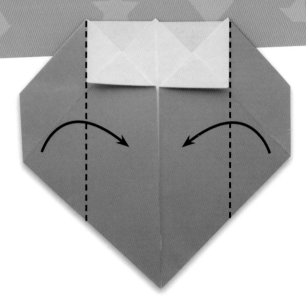

13 Valley fold the side flaps into the center.

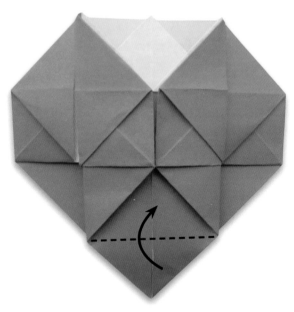

14 Valley fold the bottom to meet the two side flaps in the center.

15 Valley fold up the bottom.

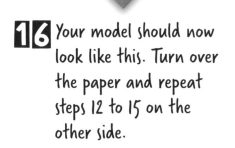

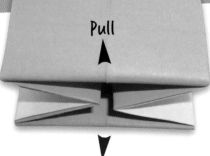

Pull

Pull

16 Your model should now look like this. Turn over the paper and repeat steps 12 to 15 on the other side.

17 Your model should now look like this.

18 Turn your model around so that the opening is at the top. Gently prise open the sides to create your container. Flatten the base with your fingers.

Tuck

Close-up of side pocket.

19 Fold down the side flaps and tuck them neatly into the side pockets.

20
You now have a standing container in which you can store lots of things!

Little Basket

This cute basket will make a great storage container for small things such as hair bands and bobby pins.

START WITH YOUR PAPER COLORED SIDE DOWN

Cute!

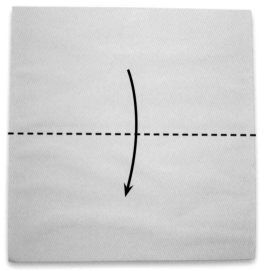

1 To make the handle, valley fold the paper in half, crease well, then unfold.

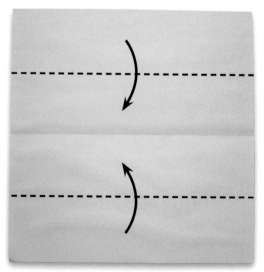

2 Valley fold the top and bottom sides into the center.

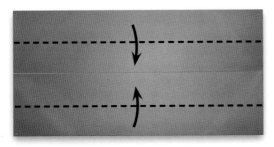

3 Valley fold the top and bottom sides again into the center.

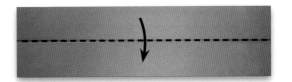

4 Valley fold the paper in half. Crease well.

5 Valley fold the paper in half again.

6 You now have your basket handle. Put it aside until step 10.

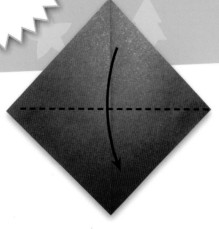

7 To make the basket, turn your base so the open ends are at the top. Valley fold the top flap in half to the bottom.

8 Valley fold the flap up again to the center.

9 Turn the model over and repeat steps 7 and 8 on the other side.

Slide

10 Slide one side of the handle into the center of the small triangles as far as it will go.

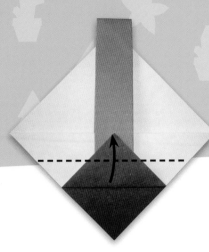

11 Holding the handle firmly in place, fold the small triangle flap and the handle up to the center fold.

12 Turn over the paper and repeat steps 10 and 11 on the other side.

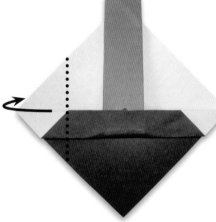

13 Mountain fold the upper left side in half so that the point touches the inside crease.

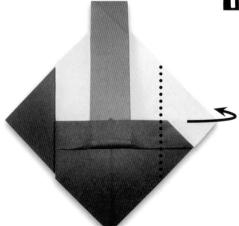

14 Do the same on the upper right side.

15 Turn over the paper and repeat steps 13 and 14 on this side.

Pull

16 Now pull out the top left flap—be very careful!

17 Fold the flap down and in, to meet the bottom flap.

18 Repeat steps 16 and 17 on the right side.

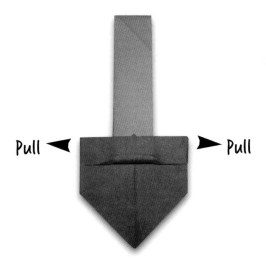

Pull ◄ ► **Pull**

19 Carefully pull the left and right flaps to open up the basket.

20 Use your fingers to gently smooth out the base of the basket.

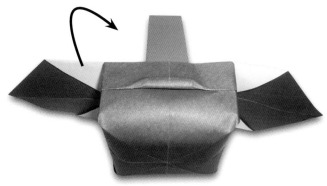

21 The model should now look like this. Fold the left flap into the basket base.

22 Smooth the left flap down and then fold the right flap in and smooth down.

23 Fill your little basket with bobby pins, marbles, or anything else you like!

Glossary

base A simple, folded shape that is used as the starting point for many different origami projects.

blintz base An origami shape named after a thin pancake and formed by folding all four corners of a square to the center.

mountain fold An origami step where a piece of paper is folded so that the crease is pointing upward, like a mountain.

pleat A fold made by doubling material back on itself.

stationery A selection of writing materials such as paper, pens, pencils, and clips.

step fold A mountain fold and a valley fold next to each other.

valley fold An origami step where a piece of paper is folded so that the crease is pointing downward, like a valley.

Further Reading

Decorative Origami Boxes by Rich Beech (Dover, 2007)
My First Origami Book by Susan Akass (CICO Kidz, 2011)
Origami for Children by Mari Ono (CICO Books, 2009)
Origami Kit for Dummies by Nick Robinson (John Wiley & Sons, 2008)

Web Sites

www.origami-instructions.com/origami-boxes-and-containers.html This web site contains instructions for a wide variety of origami containers.
www.origami-fun.com This web site is devoted to all things origami and features instructions to create paper boxes, animals, toys and much more!

Index